LUCKY LEOPARDS!

And More True Stories of Amazing Animal Rescues

SCHOLASTIC INC.

ISBN 978-0-545-72612-2

12 11 10 9 8 7 6 5 4 3 2 1   14 15 16 17 18 19/0

Printed in Vietnam   146

First Scholastic printing, March 2014

Staff for This Book
Becky Baines, *Project Editor*
Eva Absher-Schantz, *Art Director*
Kelley Miller, *Senior Photo Editor*
Ruthie Thompson, *Designer*
Ariane Szu-Tu, *Editorial Assistant*
Callie Broaddus, *Design Production Assistant*

Table of CONTENTS

Runa and Kata explore the forest. Their spotted coats blend in with the leaves.

RUNA AND KATA: LUCKY LEOPARDS

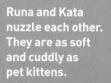

Runa and Kata
nuzzle each other.
They are as soft
and cuddly as
pet kittens.

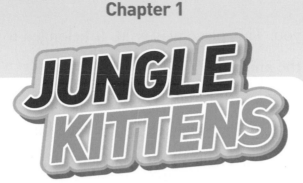

Chapter 1

March 2009, Assam, India

People watched their step in the Assam (sounds like ah-SAHM) jungle in northeast India. Roads were few and made of dirt. Trees grew so close together they almost touched. And bushy plants and fallen logs covered the forest floor. You never knew when a hungry tiger or slithering python might surprise you. This place was wild. It belonged to the animals.

Two of those animals lay sleeping in a hollow tree. They were newborn kittens, or cubs. Their mother had left them alone while she went hunting for food. The cubs should have been safe. Except before the mama returned, some woodcutters came.

The woodcutters lived in a village on the edge of the forest, in a part of India called Kokrajhar (sounds like co-kruh-JAR). They earned money by gathering firewood to sell. One man saw the hollow tree. He chopped it down with his ax. The tree landed with a thud. Then he got a big surprise.

Two tiny furballs bounced out! The startled woodcutter dropped his ax. He scooped up the tiny cats. They mewed softly. Their gray spotted coats felt as soft as a baby chick. *What are they?* the man wondered. *Baby tigers or baby leopards?*

It didn't matter. The cubs were adorable. And there was no danger in picking them up. The babies' eyes hadn't even opened yet. *If only I could sell these cats*, he thought.

The woodcutter was very poor. He knew that wild-animal dealers would pay big money for the cubs. Then the dealers would sell the cubs for even more money. Rich collectors from other countries paid thousands of dollars for wild animals to put in their backyard zoos.

Even if no dealers came along, the cubs were a good find. Maybe the woodcutter could sell them as pets. Or his neighbors might buy them. Some men tied animal parts to their swords. This was a custom, or tradition, in his village. Some people hung animal skins up to decorate their huts. Local healers also used animal parts to make medicine.

The woodcutter knew it was wrong to capture wild animals. It was wrong to sell them too. The Indian government had laws against these things. But the thought of all the money he could make dazzled him. What if he could make $200 selling the cubs? That would be like winning the lottery! With that much money he could feed his family for many months.

The woodcutter carried the cubs home. Then he quietly spread the word. He had jungle cats for sale.

But his plan went wrong. He didn't know how to take care of the cubs. He didn't know how to feed them. Or even what to feed them! Another villager became worried. He told a forest department worker named Akhim (sounds like ah-KEEM) about the cubs. Akhim went to the woodcutter. He demanded the kittens. The woodcutter turned them over.

Akhim rushed the baby cats to the local wildlife rescue center. It was run by the Wildlife Trust of India. It was not a moment too soon. The cubs hadn't eaten in days. "One of them was seriously sick," says Sonali Ghosh (sounds like so-NAH-lee GOUSH). Sonali is an officer with the Indian Forest Service. "I was scared it might die," she said.

The rescue center veterinarians (sounds like vet-er-ih-NARE-ee-ens) examined the baby cats. "These are common leopards," the vets decided. The common leopard is the kind most "commonly" seen. There are also snow leopards, clouded leopards, and Sunda clouded leopards.

Everyone at the rescue center treated the cubs with great care. Workers fed the kittens around the clock. They gave them goat's milk, using baby bottles.

Leopards are meat-eaters. So the vets wanted the cubs to get a taste for meat. After about three weeks, the workers started mixing liver soup in with the goat's milk.

The cubs ate a lot. They grew fast. As they got bigger, the markings on their coats became easier to see. One day the vets noticed something very interesting. The spots on these cubs looked different from the spots on common leopards. They were darker and grayer.

The vets looked at each other. They wondered . . .

Could it be?

Yes! These cubs weren't common leopards after all. They were clouded leopards. Extremely rare, almost never seen, clouded leopards!

Which Is Which?

Clouded leopards and common leopards are both big cats. But they are not the same kind, or species (sounds like SPEE-sheez), of cat. They are as different from each other as lions are from tigers.

COMMON LEOPARDS

- Live in forests, plains, deserts, and mountains in parts of Africa, Central Asia, India, and China.
- Roar loudly.
- Weigh up to 106 pounds (48 kg).
- Are covered with small, dark-colored, round spots.
- Have feet that always face front.

COMMON LEOPARD

CLOUDED LEOPARD

CLOUDED LEOPARDS

- Live in tropical forests in Southeast Asia and India.
- Purr and meow.
- Weigh up to 50 pounds (22.7 kg).
- Are covered with large spots that look like brown and gray clouds.
- Can turn their hind feet so they face backward.

The higher the better for clouded leopard cubs! They play, eat, and rest up in the treetops.

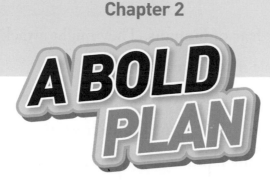

Chapter 2

A BOLD PLAN

Clouded leopards are very shy. They spend a lot of their time high up in trees. They are rarely seen in the wild.

The fact that these rescued cubs were clouded leopards changed everything. If they had been common leopards, the vets would have had to send them to a zoo. It's the law in India. That's because hand-raised common leopards lose their fear of humans. They might attack people if they were set free.

But clouded leopards don't bother humans. They hang out in treetops. Releasing hand-raised clouded leopards back into the wild would be OK. It would not put humans at risk.

But could these animals make it without their mother? Could they learn to protect themselves? Could they find their own food?

Bhaskar Choudhury (sounds like bas-CAR CHOW-durry) thought they could. So did Ian Robinson. Bhaskar is a veterinarian with the Wildlife Trust of India (WTI). Ian is the animal rescue director at the International Fund for Animal Welfare (IFAW). There was only one problem. IFAW had successfully released hand-raised elephants, bears, and even a tiger. But not a clouded leopard. No one had ever tried doing that.

The animal experts at WTI talked to the people at IFAW. They discussed what needed to be done. They talked about what could go wrong. Guess what? They decided to go for it! Everyone was super-excited to help save these rare animals.

Bhaskar and another vet, Panjit Basumatary (sounds like pan-JEET bo-SOM-uh-terry), went right to work. They put up a large cage out in the yard. They put blankets inside the cage for the cubs to sleep on. They also put branches inside it for the cubs to climb on.

Both of the cubs were males. The vets named one of them Runa (sounds like

RU-nuh). They called the other cub Kata (sounds like co-TAH).

The cubs had a lot to learn. After a few weeks, the vets started feeding them small chunks of cooked meat. Ian liked the cubs' reaction. "They would grab a piece of food and climb up in the branches to eat it," he says. "Climbing was instinctive [sounds like in-STINK-tiv] for them." In other words, they were born climbers.

The next step was getting them to eat their meat raw. That's what leopards do in the wild. So the vets began tossing dead chickens into the cubs' cage. Soon the cubs were eating plenty of raw meat.

In September 2009, Runa and Kata turned seven months old. They were big and healthy. They were eating well. It was time for them to learn clouded leopard ways. It was time to move them back to the jungle. But would the experiment work? Nobody knew.

Three men from Kokrajhar served as the cubs' keepers in the forest. They lived in huts they built themselves. The huts

were high above the ground. Each one was fitted between four trees. The huts had a bamboo floor, roof, and walls.

It was not easy work. Countless insects buzzed and whined all day and all night. They flew into the men's eyes and bit their skin. Cobras and other deadly snakes hid under bushes.

Mystery Cat

Clouded leopards are so seldom seen that scientists know very little about them. Here's what they do know:

1. Clouded leopards have very long tails, which help them balance on tree branches.
2. They use their hind feet to hang upside down from tree branches.
3. They eat birds, monkeys, pigs, small deer, and porcupines.
4. They ambush prey by leaping onto their backs and biting their necks.
5. They are good swimmers.
6. They are called "mint leopards" in China and "tree tigers" in Malaysia.

The keepers also faced danger from prowling tigers and charging elephants. That's why they put their huts up high—to stay out of the animals' reach.

For nine long months, the keepers lived like this. "These men were dedicated to these cubs," says Ian. "And brave. This was a tough job."

The keepers took turns, so that two men were on duty at the same time. The third would have the week off to return to the village for food and supplies.

Runa and Kata also slept in the treetops. They needed to be safe from tigers and elephants, too. Their keepers lashed bamboo poles together and built a platform high off the ground. They built a ladder the same way. Then they set a large green cage on top of the platform. The cage was made of metal and wire. It had a swinging door that locked. The keepers climbed up the ladder each night and locked the cubs inside.

During the day the keepers took the cubs for long walks on the ground. They walked them each morning and evening. The keepers kept the cubs on a leash at first. This way the cubs slowly got used to the sights, sounds, and smells of the forest.

At first the young leopards were scared. This was natural and to be expected. But after a week, the keepers let the cubs loose. They expected them to run around exploring. Instead, Runa and Kata acted like pet dogs. They stuck close to their keepers.

The vets and keepers began to worry. "The animal that goes off and cares nothing for you when he goes is most successful," says Ian. Had these cubs become too fond of people?

If so, that was bad news. Humans are the clouded leopard's biggest enemy. They hunt and trap the cats for their fur and bones. If these cubs liked people, they would leave the forest. They would hang around the villages looking for food and friendship. That kind of behavior would get them killed.

Raising these clouded leopards had been a grand experiment. But now it seemed they had failed. Bhaskar, Ian, and the others felt like a big black cloud had settled over their heads.

One of the twins peers through the bushes. His black markings, pink nose, and white muzzle look painted on.

Chapter 3

TOUGH LOVE

The cubs' forest keepers knew they had to do something. They decided to change their behavior toward the cubs. One day Kata stopped walking to scratch his nails on a fallen log. Afterward he rubbed against his keeper like a house cat.

The keeper sighed. His heart told him to pet and snuggle Kata. But his head told him he must not.

Not if he wanted the cat to stay in the wild. Not if he wanted Kata to survive! The keeper knew Kata needed to become independent. So Kata's faithful human friend forced himself to do something very hard. He turned Kata around and pushed him away.

Again and again the keepers did this. Soon the plan seemed to be working. The cubs began grabbing chunks of food and scrambling up a tree. The keepers were pleased. At least they were until the cats shot straight up a towering tree trunk. They climbed so high that the keepers had to crane their necks to see them. Now what? Would the spunky daredevils suddenly turn into scaredy cats? Would they be afraid to come down?

Not to worry. The clouded leopards simply turned their bodies and spun their hind feet around. They dug their sharp claws into the tree's bark. And bingo! They raced headfirst to the ground!

What a neat trick! Squirrels can do that. But tigers can't. Neither can lions or common leopards. Clouded leopards are the only big cats that can.

Runa and Kata gradually learned their way around the forest. So their keepers let them stay loose for longer. But the keepers still followed the cats everywhere they went. If the cubs disappeared, their keepers whistled. The cats ran back.

How to travel through the forest was not all these furry twins needed to learn. They also needed to learn to hunt.

In the wild, clouded leopard mamas bring their babies food to eat. Supper is often a golden langur (sounds like LANG-goor) monkey. Monkeys live in the trees and are easy to find. But clouded leopards also eat birds, squirrels, snakes, lizards, and big juicy insects.

As adults, clouded leopards must catch their own food. But how do they know how to do it? Do they learn by watching? Or are they born with the ability and develop it over time? Scientists are not exactly sure. "We believed that the skill of hunting was born in them," Ian says.

If he was right, the cubs could make it in the wild. If he was wrong, they would have to live in a zoo. It was time to find out.

Runa and Kata were full-grown now. In the wild, adult clouded leopards are nocturnal (sounds like nok-TUR-nul). This means they sleep during the day and hunt and prowl at night. The keepers decided to keep the twins' cage door open all the time. Now the leopards could explore whenever they wanted.

Runa and Kata started staying out later and later. But they still returned to their cage to eat. "Feeding was very rough-and-tumble," Ian says. "The cubs had to be fed in separate corners. Otherwise they would fight and steal each other's food." This went on for months. Would the leopards ever learn to hunt for themselves?

One day, a stray chicken wandered into the forest. Runa spied it and grabbed the bird by the neck. But he didn't kill it. A minute later he let it go. Still, he had taken an important first step.

The next chicken that crossed Runa's path was not so lucky. "These cats were always on the edge of their nerves," says Ian. "They were so alert and aware of the slightest sound." This chicken barely entered the forest before feathers flew. Both leopards attacked the hen. They wrestled for it. They bit. They snarled and hissed. Kata finally won the prize. Then he carried his supper straight up a tree.

Clouded leopards are the only big cats that spend so much time in trees. As Runa and Kata started to do this, they spent less time with their keepers.

Weeks passed. The leopards stayed away

longer and longer. They stopped playing with their keepers. They focused on each other instead. Runa and Kata now behaved less like pets and more like wild animals.

Then something happened that sealed the deal. In May 2010, a stray dog trotted into the forest. The keepers saw the dog coming. But they were too far away to help. All they could do was hold their breath and hope for the best.

And then it happened.

Runa and Kata teamed up and attacked the dog!

It might seem sad, but in the jungle, "kill or be killed" is a way of life. The big cats were just following their instincts.

And that's exactly what the keepers were waiting to see. Now they knew their job was done. Runa and Kata could defend themselves. They could catch their own food. And they could find their way in the forest. The keepers told Ian, Bhaskar, and Panjit that it was time to let the young cats go.

The vets came. They gave Runa and Kata medicine that put them to sleep. Then the vets put white radio-tracking collars on the cats. This way they could track them to see if they survived. If they did, the vets could release other rescued clouded leopard cubs.

Life in the wild is dangerous for clouded leopards. It is for all animals. But Runa and Kata were lucky. They got a second chance.

They were free!

One Year Later

Were the clouded leopard cubs still alive? A year after Runa and Kata were released, animal experts returned to the jungle to find out. Things looked bad at first. There were no signals from the radio collars. Elephants had destroyed the cubs' treetop cage.

But the experts kept searching. Days later, they found fresh paw prints. They found clouded leopard poop. They saw scratch marks on a tree. Then they met a forestry worker. He had seen a big spotted cat wearing a white collar. These were all very good signs that the cubs had survived!

Koa lies flat on the shore. He has an injured eye, can't move, and looks dead.

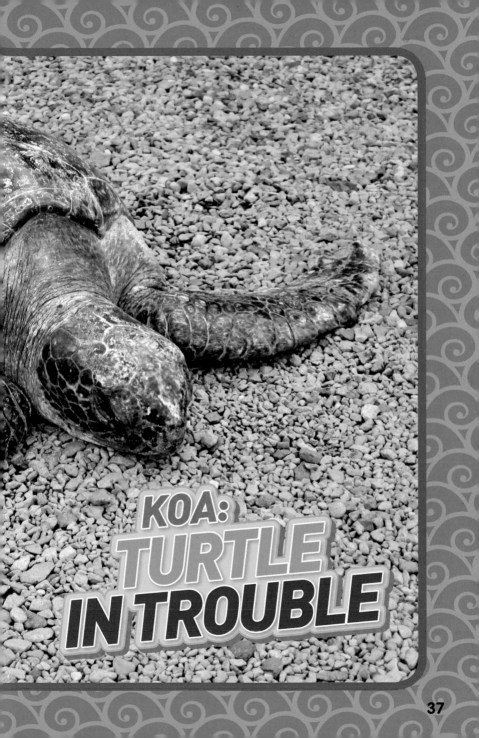

KOA:
TURTLE
IN TROUBLE

Like all green turtles, Koa has a heart-shaped shell. It's made up of flattened bones.

Chapter 1

WRONG-WAY SEA TURTLE

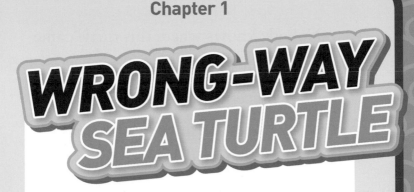

June 18, 2012, northern Oregon

A male green sea turtle needed help. He was stuck on a sandy beach along the coast. Healthy male turtles live their entire lives at sea. But this poor guy had washed in on the tide. Now he lay still. Hungry seagulls swooped and shrieked (sounds like SHREEKT) overhead. One gull had already pecked at one of the turtle's eyes.

Nobody knows where this turtle came from. Nobody knows how he landed in Oregon. Graceful swimmers like him normally live in warm tropical oceans. This fellow might have started out in warm water near Mexico. It may be that he got caught in a current. Then the fast-moving ocean water carried him north. The ocean is colder up there.

Sea turtles often ride warm ocean currents halfway around the world. But if the water turns cold, their muscles stop working. They become paralyzed (sounds like PAIR-uh-lized). The turtles can't move. They can't feed and they can't escape. This is called being "cold-stunned."

Nadine Fuller was not feeling her best either. She had been hiking and camping in California with her children and grandchildren. The family had had a wonderful time. But 70-year-old Nadine was tired. She was exhausted from lugging a backpack and all her gear.

Now she was driving back home to Forks, Washington. It was five in the afternoon. She had 800 miles (1,287 km) to go. So Nadine decided to stop for the night in Newport, Oregon. The Moolack Shores Motel there is one of her favorite places.

Nadine pulled into a parking space at the motel. Then she walked inside. "Hi, Frank," she said to the man behind the desk. "Do you have any rooms available? I'd like one for tonight."

Franklin Brooks smiled and nodded. He offered her a plate of cookies. Nadine nibbled on one while Frank checked her in. They chatted a bit. Then Nadine climbed the stairs to her room. She unlocked the door and stepped inside. She dropped her bags on the floor. She opened sliding glass doors to a balcony overlooking the ocean. "Ahh," she sighed.

Nadine breathed in the salty air and gazed out to sea. She listened to the waves pounding the shore. She looked at the Newport lighthouse across the bay. In a few hours, its light would come on. It had been a warm, sunny day. Nadine planned to settle down in a comfy deck chair and enjoy the view. Later she would watch

the sun set over the ocean. She was ready
to relax!

But while she was still standing, Nadine
spotted something strange lying on the
beach. It was bigger than a kitchen sink.
"I thought it was a rock, at first," she says.
"But something about it did not look right."

Nadine went back inside her room.
She unpacked the binoculars she always
brings on trips. She held them to her eyes
and adjusted the focus.

Wow! It was a sea turtle!

Nadine volunteers with an
environmental (sounds like in-vi-run-
MENT-ul) group called Beachwatchers.
She patrols the beach near her home
once a month looking for dead birds.
If she finds any, she reports them to

Beachwatchers. A rise in numbers tells the group there has been an oil spill or some other disaster in or near the ocean. Nadine had spotted many kinds of birds over the years. She had seen puffins, cormorants (sounds like KORM-er-ents), loons, and albatross (sounds like AL-buh-tross).

She also had seen sea turtles swimming in the ocean off California. But she had never seen a sea turtle this far north. And she had never seen one stranded, or stuck, on shore. "Suddenly, I wasn't tired anymore," says Nadine. Clutching her binoculars, she scurried down the stairs and out onto the beach.

But when Nadine reached the turtle her joy faded. The animal wasn't moving.

Nadine walked all around the turtle.

Race to the Sea

The most dangerous time in a green turtle's life is right after it hatches. That's because green turtle mothers don't protect their young. They simply drag themselves up on a beach, dig a hole, and lay 100 to 200 eggs. The turtle moms cover the eggs with sand. Then they return to the ocean.

The eggs hatch all at once. The first thing the newborn turtles do is scramble toward the water. Along the way, birds and crabs eat many of them. But those that do make it to the ocean can live for 80 years.

She snapped several pictures of it. Then she gently scraped the sand from the creature's face with a stick. "He blinked one eye," she says. "But I thought that was only a reflex. I thought the turtle was dead."

Some people might have tried to put the turtle back in the water. But Nadine remembered her training. Beachwatchers had taught her to report and not touch.

She knew better than to try to do anything herself. She hurried back to the motel.

"Frank," she cried to the innkeeper. "I found a sea turtle lying on the beach!" She showed him the photos on her digital camera.

Did You Know?

Green turtles sometimes crawl out of the water to sunbathe on land.

Frank looked wide-eyed. "I know the head of marine mammal stranding," he said. "His office is only three miles from here."

Frank dialed Jim Rice's cell phone. But Jim was not at his office. He was home cooking supper when his cell phone rang.

"There's a dead turtle on the beach," Frank told him.

Jim felt sad that the turtle had died. But a dead animal was no reason to hurry. Jim figured he could take his time. He finished fixing supper for his ten-year-old son. He ate a bit himself. His wife arrived home. And then, *rrring!* His phone rang again.

"You know that turtle I told you about?" Frank said. "Well, it just moved!"

Randy Getman carries Koa up the stairs from the beach. Jim Rice (left) and Franklin Brooks (right) help.

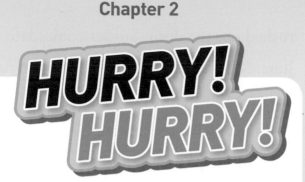

HURRY! HURRY!

Jim Rice switched into emergency mode. "There are seven species of sea turtles," he says. "And they are all endangered." This means that they are so few in number that they may one day become extinct. "If we find a live sea turtle," Jim says, "we do everything we can to get him back out there."

It was seven at night when Jim

rushed out the door. Sunset comes late in June. Maybe he could still rescue the turtle before dark. But he had to hurry.

Jim drove to the beach. He swung his car into the parking lot and ran down to the sand. Frank was standing there beside a large turtle. Jim approached the turtle and lightly touched its neck. The turtle's head twitched. Frank had been right. This turtle was alive.

Jim was a marine mammal researcher at Hatfield Marine Science Center. He spent his days studying dead animals found on Oregon's beaches. Most of these were whales, seals, sea lions, or porpoises. It was Jim's job to figure out why they died.

Before moving out west, Jim had worked in Massachusetts. He rescued and helped hundreds of sea turtles recover there. He was a sea turtle expert. But he had not rescued a single one since moving to Oregon. All the turtles Jim worked on there were dead.

Jim examined the turtle's eyes. They looked sunken in. This was a sure sign of dehydration (sounds like de-hi-DRAY-shun). This means the animal didn't have enough water in his body. Green turtles do not drink water. They get all the liquid they need from the food they eat. But this turtle couldn't dive or feed. He was paralyzed. Jim could tell the animal was cold-stunned.

The turtle was in very bad shape. Two more hours on the beach, and he would die for sure. "I faced a challenge," Jim says. "It was getting darker. And the tide was coming in. Somehow we had to beat it." Otherwise, the rushing water would sweep the helpless turtle back out to sea. It would surely drown.

Jim also faced another problem. He didn't have his work truck with him. His work truck had big tires. Big tires would let him drive on the sandy beach. But all he had was his station wagon. Driving to work to fetch his truck would take too long. It would be dark when he returned. And it would be high tide.

So how was he going to get this big animal off the beach? Jim and Frank were discussing what to do when Randy Getman appeared. Randy was the general manager at the Moolack Shores Motel.

He was big and strong, and he loved
animals. Randy had an idea. "I'll carry
him to your car," he said.

"You'll what?" said Jim. "This turtle
must weigh 130 pounds [59 kg]. You'll
hurt your back."

Randy shook his head. "I can do it,"
he insisted.

So Jim called
James Burke. James is
director of animal
husbandry (sounds
like HUZ-ben-dree) at
the Oregon Coast

Did You Know?

Green turtles eat
jellyfish. This surprised
scientists. Until 2009,
they thought these
turtles ate only plants.

Aquarium. Jim told James about the turtle
and asked if the aquarium had room for
him. "Of course," James said. "I'll meet
you there."

Turtle Trivia

GREEN SEA TURTLES

- Have flippers instead of legs. The bones in their flippers look like the bones in your hands.
- Cannot pull their heads inside their shells.
- Can stay underwater for hours without coming up to breathe.
- Have no teeth.
- Weigh up to 500 pounds (227 kg).
- Swim very fast, up to 20 miles (32 km) an hour.
- Have brown or black shells. They get their name from the green-colored fat inside their bodies.

Jim put his phone away. He and Randy stood on opposite sides of the turtle. They gripped his shell and lifted him up. Frank stood behind, holding some of the weight. The three men carried the turtle down the beach and up the first set of stairs. But then the stairs narrowed. The men could no longer walk side by side. They set the turtle down and rested a few minutes.

Then Randy bent over. "Put him on," he said.

Jim and Frank lifted the turtle onto Randy's back. They draped the turtle's flippers over Randy's strong shoulders. And Randy piggybacked the turtle up two more flights of stairs.

In the parking lot, Jim opened his car's hatchback. He and Frank lifted the turtle off Randy's shoulders and set him inside. Jim shut the hatch, hopped in the driver's seat, and headed to the aquarium. The fishy stink of turtle grew stronger as he drove.

Jim called James Burke again on the way. "We'll be there in ten minutes," he said.

When Jim and the turtle arrived, James was waiting at the door. He and Jim unloaded the turtle and carried him into a large, warehouse-type building. Inside the building sat different-size water tanks. The men found an empty one and laid the turtle inside. They propped the edges of his shell on foam pads to keep weight off his lungs. That way his chest could go in and out with every breath.

Big as the turtle was, he was too weak to put up a fight. That made him easy to handle. Jim and James knew what to do, and they worked quickly. First they checked the turtle over. Could he move his flippers and blink his eyes? Barely. They weighed the turtle and washed the few wounds he had. Then they took his temperature (sounds like TEM-preh-chur). Next, they drew blood and injected fluids into the turtle's body.

"It was pretty intense," says James. "This turtle belonged to an endangered species. If we saved him, and put him back in the wild, we'd help his whole species survive."

But could he be saved?

The two men did not know. All they could do was try their hardest. The rest was up to nature . . . and the turtle.

Green turtles swim fast. They can zip along at 20 miles (32 km) an hour.

Chapter 3

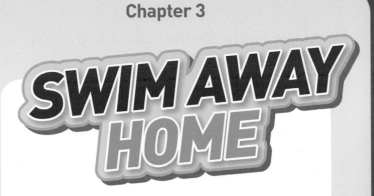

SWIM AWAY HOME

At first, it was touch and go. James Burke kept the turtle dry. He took his temperature daily. He wanted the turtle's body temperature, or temp, to match the air temp of the room. It took two weeks for that to happen. When it did, James added a little water to the tank. Then he began raising the water temp. He set it two degrees higher each day.

At last James got the turtle's body temp up to 75°F (24°C). That was a nice, healthy temp.

James and his co-workers had to get the turtle eating next. They fed him water plants called algae (sounds like AL-jee). They also fed him a kind of seaweed called bull kelp. They gave the turtle tiny bits at first.

"We were very careful," says James. "Sea turtles get tossed around in the surf. They get water in their lungs. So they often suffer from pneumonia [sounds like nu-MOAN-yuh.]" That's a lung sickness. A rescued turtle can seem to get

Did You Know?

Green sea turtle eggs are the size of Ping-Pong balls. Newly hatched turtles are about two inches (5 cm) long.

better. Then it can suddenly die of the disease. James had seen it happen.

In time, the keepers moved the turtle to a larger tank. Then they began dropping more algae into the water for him to munch on. "By week three, things were starting to look really good," James says. "This guy just wasn't giving up."

The keepers grew fond of the big reptile. One of them named him Koa (sounds like CO-uh). Koa is a Hawaiian word. It means strong and fearless.

By August 21, Koa had gained 28 pounds (13 kg). He acted very lively now. James knew he could be returned to the ocean. But not in Oregon. The water there was much too cold. Koa needed to go south. But where? And how?

James called the United States Fish and Wildlife Service. Together they decided that San Diego, California, looked good. It was 780 miles (1,255 km) to the south. The ocean temp there was in the high 70s (about 25°C) in the summer. And SeaWorld San Diego was there. SeaWorld helped many sick and hurt marine animals get well. They had the equipment and know-how for the job. Plus, the United States Navy had an airbase in San Diego. Maybe they could help. And that's exactly what they did.

A Navy plane flew from San Diego to Eugene (sounds like yu-JEEN), Oregon. On board were two animal keepers from SeaWorld. Koa was waiting for them at the airport. He was in a large wooden crate.

Where Did All the Turtles Go?

Five hundred years ago, the ocean near Florida teemed with turtles. There were so many that one sailor said the ocean "seemed to be full of little rocks." Then over the years things changed. People stole turtle eggs. Large fishing nets captured turtles by accident. People put buildings over beaches where turtles nested. Green turtles began to disappear.

In 1978, scientists listed green turtles as endangered. And people took action! Florida set aside 30.5 miles (49 km) of beach just for turtles. Today more green turtles nest there than anywhere else in the United States.

The crate was handmade by workers at the Oregon Coast Aquarium. On it were stickers reading "This Side Up." It was lined with foam-rubber padding. Twenty airholes were drilled in its sides. Each airhole was as big as a silver dollar.

When the plane set down at the airport in Eugene, a crowd was waiting. Everyone wanted to see what the Navy and SeaWorld called "Operation Turtle Lift." Reporters were there with cameras and recorders. Even Nadine Fuller was there. She was excited to see the turtle she had found. The last time she saw him he was near death. Now he was healthy again. It gave Nadine a good feeling to know that Koa would be released to cruise around the seaweed again.

She watched the keepers load Koa on board. Then the plane lifted off. "Good luck," she whispered. "I'm glad I was the one to find and help you."

Most stranded sea turtles need a full year of care. But Koa got well fast. By the end of September, he was ready to be released. The only problem left was the time of year. It was fall. The ocean was cold. But in October, the coastal waters turned surprisingly warm. They were warm enough for Koa to survive. His keepers attached a small ID tag to one of his flippers. They wanted to know if he ever washed ashore again.

SeaWorld workers put Koa on a special boat. It had a door in one side. They drove the turtle out to sea. Then they opened the

Did You Know?

A green turtle's shell is supertough. Not even a shark can bite through it.

door. They pushed the turtle into the waves. Koa stroked his powerful front flippers and glided away.

The release team cheered.

People in Oregon also cheered. They were glad to hear the good news about Koa. Very few sea turtles strand on the Oregon coast. Even fewer survive. It's just too cold. But there was something odd about 2012. Seven sea turtles stranded in Oregon that year.

"It was the most strandings in a single year that I have on record," says Jim Rice. He doesn't know why. Maybe a freak warm water current brought the turtles north and then suddenly turned cold.

But there is no proof of that. What Jim does know is that Koa is the only one of those seven stranded turtles to survive.

It took months of work. It also took dozens of people: Nadine Fuller, Franklin Brooks, Jim Rice, Randy Getman, James Burke and the staff at the Oregon Coast Aquarium, the U.S. Fish and Wildlife Service, SeaWorld San Diego, and the Navy. Together they gave the plucky green turtle a new life.

Koa's rescuers hope that he will live long. They also hope he will father many thousands of babies. Maybe he will help green sea turtles come off the endangered list. If so, these gentle creatures will continue to fill our oceans. And we will be happier just knowing they are there.

CROOKED NECK: THE LONE LOON

This loon has caught a fish. Before eating, he'll turn it so it goes down headfirst.

A loon sits on her nest. Most loons use the same nest year after year.

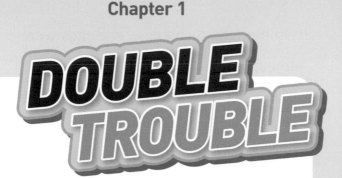

July 2009, Old Forge, New York

Few people slowed down long enough to notice. But a bird called a common loon sat on a muddy nest in a busy lake called First Lake. It is one of a chain of lakes in the Adirondack (sounds like Ad-i-RON-dack) Mountains.

The loon had a black head, snow white breast, and white spots on black wings. Inside her nest lay two big, greenish eggs. The eggs were almost ready to hatch.

But before they did, a storm struck. Rain poured down. The water level in the lake quickly rose much higher than normal. Then the sun came out. Waves from passing boats washed over the nest.

The loon and her mate had made a mistake. They had built their nest on a floating bog. A floating bog is a chunk of matted grass, roots, and moss that is not connected to the shore. It looks like a little island, but there's no solid ground. Floating bogs act like sponges. They soak up water.

A loon-watcher named Bob Zimmerman knew about the nest. He grew concerned when the waters rose. So he jumped into his canoe and paddled over to check. *Oh, no!* he thought. Bob rushed back to camp—which is what he calls his summer home near the lake—and called Gary Lee. Gary is a retired forest ranger and an expert on birds.

"We have some loons here that need your help," Bob said. "Their nest is flooded!"

"I'll be right there," Gary said. He raced outside. Sitting out in his yard was a nesting platform he had built for emergencies. It was made of unsinkable cedar logs, Styrofoam (STI-ruh-foam), and plastic mesh. Gary lifted the platform into the back of his pickup truck. He drove to Bob's camp.

Gary knew he didn't have much time. If a little water seeps into their nest, loon eggs can survive for a short while. But more than a half inch (1.3 cm) of water will chill the eggs, and the chicks will die.

When Gary reached Bob's camp, he found Bob and his son-in-law waiting for him. The three men hopped into Bob's rowboat and rowed to the nest. The sight of them frightened the mother loon. "She panicked," Gary says. She slid headfirst into the water and watched the goings-on from a short distance away.

Gary and Bob climbed out of the boat and onto the floating bog. It sank. Cold water rose to their waists. Gary snatched up the eggs and handed them to the man in the boat. "Keep them warm," he said.

Gary and Bob quickly pulled the loons' soggy nesting material off the bog. Then

Gary pressed the nest back together on top of his homemade platform. He tied the platform to two cement blocks and dropped it in the water. He returned the eggs to the nest. Then the men hurried away.

Mama loon jumped right back on her nest. A few days later, *hooray!* Her chicks hatched!

By December, the pair of loons and their youngsters had left the lake. This is normal. Loons migrate. They spend winters in the ocean and return to the same northern lakes each spring.

The mama loon and her mate had been coming to First Lake for several years. So had Neil and Aline Newman.

Did You Know?

Loon chicks can swim as soon as they hatch.

The Lowdown on Loons

1. In summer, loons live on northern lakes from Maine to Alaska. They winter in the oceans.
2. Loons eat fish, frogs, and bugs.
3. Loons need a runway. They beat their wings and run across the water for as long as four football fields in order to take off.
4. Loons can fly more than 75 miles (121 km) an hour.
5. Loons wail, hoot, and make a sound like crazy laughter. Each male also has a special call that is all his own.

They had a camp nearby. Every year
they watched for the loons to return. The
male loon always arrived first. Sometimes
they spotted him on the water. Other
times they heard his spooky cry.
"Aaaaahhhhhhooooooo!" he would wail,
calling for his mate. Aline and Neil would
always stop what they were doing and listen.

Now it was a warm afternoon in
September 2011. Aline and Neil were
boating on the lake. Aline spotted the
mother loon on the water. Her mate and a
new pair of chicks drifted beside her.

"Look," Aline said. "Our loons are
out." Neil followed her gaze and smiled.

The adult birds looked handsome as
always. But there was something odd
about the youngsters. One chick looked

smaller than the other. Loon eggs only hatch a day apart. So the chicks should have been about the same size. Neil and Aline didn't think much about it at first. They were too busy enjoying their pontoon (sounds like pon-TOON) boat.

A pontoon is a flat-bottomed boat built on top of metal tubes. It's like a raft. Aline had packed books, soft drinks, crackers, and cheese. It was a perfect day to lie in the sun and read.

Neil cut the motor and dropped anchor. They watched the loons while they ate. Every so often the parents poked their heads underwater and scanned for fish. When they saw one, they'd dive and grab it. One of the chicks was doing the same. But the other just floated along.

This worried Neil. "Why doesn't the smallest loon dive?" he asked. "And why does his head face backward? Does he have a crooked neck? There must be something wrong with him."

"Oh, he's okay," Aline said. "He's just smoothing his feathers with his bill." Loons do that to lock their feathers together and make them waterproof.

"Maybe," said Neil. "But he doesn't look right. I'm going to call him Crooked Neck."

Aline laughed. "That's a good name."

The two of them read until the sun sank low in the sky. Then Neil started the engine and they skimmed across the lake. They didn't know it yet, but their beloved loons now faced a different danger.

Like all loons, this one has red eyes. Red eyes help loons see better underwater.

Chapter 2

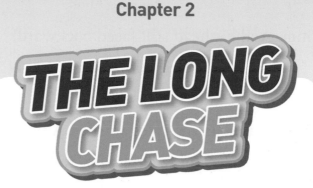

THE LONG CHASE

The next day Neil suggested they go boating again. "I want to check on Crooked Neck," he told Aline.

It took a while to find the loon. And this time Crooked Neck was all alone. Chicks older than eight weeks can catch much of their own food. So their parents sometimes leave them alone during the day. But even his sibling had deserted him. And his head still faced backward!

"I knew it," Neil said. "Something is wrong with that bird."

The tone in his voice startled Aline. This time she had to agree. But what could be the matter?

Neil steered the boat in the bird's direction. A normal loon would have dived to get away from them. Crooked Neck didn't do that. But he zigzagged around so fast that they couldn't get close. Aline and Neil chased him all over the lake. After an hour, they gave up. They settled down and tried to read. This time Aline focused on an article she had printed off the Internet. And that's when it hit her.

"Neil," she said. "You're right. That loon is in trouble, and I think I know why!"

The piece she had read told about some people who were boating in the ocean. They came upon a whale. Imagine! An enormous sperm whale was just floating there, not moving. To their surprise, the boaters saw steam coming from its blowhole. They knew it was alive.

But why was it acting so strange? A closer look revealed that the whale was hopelessly tangled in a giant fishing net.

Aline suddenly realized that Crooked Neck must be tangled up, too. Only he was tangled in fishing line.

"What should we do?" Neil asked.

Aline pulled out her cell phone. "I'll call Gary Lee," she said. "He saved the loons last time, when their eggs were underwater."

But Gary wasn't home. His wife said he was out of town. Then she added something even more upsetting.

"Somebody called about that loon before. Gary tried to help, but he couldn't catch it."

"I can see why," groaned Neil when Aline told him. "Well, we can't wait. That poor loon is suffering something terrible. We'll have to help him ourselves."

"But how? We don't even have a net."

Neil didn't answer. He just restarted the engine and took off after the loon. He and Aline spent another two hours crisscrossing the lake. No matter how fast they drove, the speedy loon stayed out of reach. It was so frustrating.

"Stop swimming, you stupid loon!" Aline wanted to scream. "We're trying to help you." Finally, they lost heart.

"It's hopeless," Aline said. Neil shrugged in defeat and aimed the boat toward camp.

They were picking up speed when Aline turned for one last look. "Stop!" she yelled, springing to her feet. "Crooked Neck is here!"

"Here? Where?" Neil turned off the engine and ran to the back of the boat. He and Aline both peered over the side. Neither of them could believe what they saw. Crooked Neck had swum right up to them. He was almost close enough to touch. And sure enough, there was a green nylon fishing line trailing behind him.

"What changed his mind?" Aline wondered. "Why did he come to us?"

Neil shook his head in astonishment. "He must be getting weak. Maybe he saw us leaving and thought we were his last chance." Neil reached his hand back. "Quick. Give me the paddle."

Aline handed him the wooden canoe paddle they kept on the boat for emergencies. He stuck the paddle under the fishing line and lifted it up toward himself. Then he grabbed the line, dropped the paddle, and pulled in the loon. Once the loon was within reach, Neil grabbed his legs. Crooked Neck was upside down when Neil brought him into the boat. But Neil immediately shifted the loon to an upright position.

Oooo hahahaha!

What on earth? A loon suddenly rears up and flaps its wings. Then it runs on the water. Really! You might even hear its webbed feet slapping the water's surface. The crazy-acting bird also shrieks. It sounds like a wicked witch laughing.

Loons do this if anything—animal or human—comes close to their nest. They're trying to protect their eggs. These weird-sounding calls might not scare you in daytime. But a loon's cries can sound pretty spooky after dark.

Crooked Neck was scared now.
He nipped Neil on the back of his hand.
"Ouch!" he cried.

Had the loon bitten Aline, she probably
would have dropped it. But Neil grew up
on a farm. He had handled chickens.
He never let go.

Aline wrapped the bird in her beach
towel. Then she pinned him down on the
back seat so they could examine him.
What they saw made them feel sick.
The animal was tied up like a ball of
yarn. Green fishing line encircled his
legs, body, and one wing. He couldn't
move his head. His long, black beak
was tied shut with his tongue hanging
out one side. No way could he call
or eat!

How long had Crooked Neck been like this?

Neil dug out the cheese knife Aline had packed in their lunch. Aline held the bird down, while he sawed away at the tough nylon line. But the knife was too dull to make the cut.

"Keep a tight hold," Neil said. "We'll take the loon back to camp, where we have better tools." Neil returned to the driver's seat and started up the boat.

The wind blew Aline's hair as they shot across the water. Meanwhile, the loon flapped and squirmed beneath her hands. He was not fully grown. But he already weighed more than their cat. And he was strong.

"I can't hold him," Aline yelled. "He's going to get away!"

Neil Newman lifts Crooked Neck into the boat. The loon's head is tied to one side by fishing line.

Chapter 3

It was a struggle, but somehow Aline hung onto the loon while Neil drove. They were zipping along when Neil spotted another boat up ahead. It had the word "Sheriff" painted on the side. Neil waved and headed straight for it. Once there, he cut the motor and the boat began rocking. Deputy Sheriff Russ Brombacher (sounds like BROM-bock-er) reached over and steadied it with his hands. That kept the two crafts from colliding. "What's the trouble?" Russ asked.

"Do you have a knife?" Neil said. "We have a loon wrapped up in fishing line. We need a sharp knife to cut him free."

Russ pulled a rope out of a storage bin and threw it to Neil. Neil used it to tie the two boats together. Then the deputy scrambled aboard. He handed Neil a folding knife with a broad, sharp blade. Neil nodded. "This will do it," he said.

Aline held the loon's body. The deputy held the bird's head. Neil slid the knife blade under a loop of line wrapped around the bird's beak. He sawed upward, being careful to avoid the loon's dried-out tongue. It looked brittle enough to break.

Neil finally removed the fishing line from around Crooked Neck's beak. But there was still a length of it hanging out of his throat. Neil tugged. More line came out. He tugged some more and line kept coming. It was like unwinding thread from a spool.

This all started with fishing line left in the lake. Maybe a fisherman baited his hook and cast his line, but his line broke. Or maybe his hook snagged. Unable to jerk it free, the fisherman cut off his line. Later a fish ate the bait. Now the fish was attached to the line. Then Crooked Neck ate the fish.

When Crooked Neck felt fishing line dangling from his mouth, he tried to get rid of it. He pointed his beak to the sky and flung his head around. But this only made things worse. The line wrapped around the loon's beak and wing. The more Crooked Neck struggled, the more tied up he got.

Neil kept pulling and two metal sinkers, or weights, emerged from deep inside the loon's belly. The last thing to come out was a rusty fishhook.

Aline turned the loon on his side and unwrapped the towel. Neil cut away the line from around the bird's wing. Untangling the loon had taken half an hour. But they did it. Crooked Neck was free! Neil scooped him up and tossed him over the side.

Kersplash! The loon hit the water. For a second, he just sat there. Then he turned his head to the left. He turned it to the right. He stretched his neck. It wasn't bent anymore. The excited loon flapped his wings and stood up on the water. *"Aaaaaaaahhhhhhhooooooooo!"* he wailed. The familiar call carried over the waves. But this time it sounded almost joyful. Was Crooked Neck telling his parents he was okay? Then he dived! And dived again! And dived some more!

The newly freed loon celebrated like a baseball player who had just won the World Series. Watching him brought tears of joy to Aline's eyes.

Did You Know?

Loons can live to be 25 to 30 years old.

Neil turned to the deputy. "Thank you," he said and shook his hand.

Death Trap

This is the fishing line that caught Crooked Neck. It's made of nylon. If left in water, it will last 600 years. This bad stuff will clog up our lakes, rivers, and oceans. Countless waterbirds, turtles, and fish get caught in fishing line. Most of them will die.

But you can help. Buy biodegradable (sounds like bi-o-dih-GRADE-uh-bul) fishing line. It's made of corn! It rots away in only five years. Compare prices. Nylon line costs $5 a spool. A spool of biodegradable line costs $10. The good feeling you get from saving animals? That is worth millions!

Russ Brombacher grinned. "Glad I could help." He took back his knife and returned to his boat.

Aline and Neil felt like celebrating, too. They drove their boat around for an hour laughing and reliving their adventure. Then Neil asked, "Want to go back and see Crooked Neck again?"

"Yes!" Aline answered. They happily returned to where they had released the loon. But their spirits burst the moment they found him. Crooked Neck was in the one place a healthy loon should never be. He was sitting on shore! Loons avoid land because they can't walk well. They are much better at flying and swimming.

"Maybe we should catch him again and take him to a vet," Aline suggested.

Neil climbed out of the boat. His heart was heavy as he trudged barefoot through the sand. Then, surprise! The alert loon suddenly waddled to the water and swam away.

Neil beamed. "He's heading toward Dog Island," he said. "He's looking for his family."

It was Sunday night. Neil and Aline headed home as well. They had to work on Monday. But the next Saturday morning they took the boat back to check on their loon. The first time they circled the lake, Crooked Neck was nowhere to be found. The Newmans' thoughts turned gloomy. Was Crooked Neck still alive?

They started around again. And then they saw them. Their loons swam out of the marsh.

One, two, three . . . Aline sucked in her breath as she counted. There were four loons!

Neil reached over and squeezed Aline's hand. "So he did survive."

Crooked Neck would need to eat a lot to get as big as his sibling. But he had time. Nearly two months remained before the lake would freeze over. The only question still bothering Aline and Neil was whether Crooked Neck could handle food. Would his damaged tongue prevent him from eating?

They watched and waited. Then they saw something really special. One of

Crooked Neck's parents caught a fish . . . and gave it to him. Gulp! He sent it down the hatch.

Neil grinned and raised his hand in the air. "Mission accomplished," he said.

Aline grinned back and slapped him five. The happy feelings she had from helping that loon are still with her now.

THE END

Guess what? Aline Alexander Newman is not only the author of this book, she also took part in this story! Aline and her husband, Neil, helped save Crooked Neck from the fishing line in September of 2011.

DON'T MISS!

NATIONAL GEOGRAPHIC KiDS CHAPTERS

COURAGEOUS CANINE!

And More True Stories of Amazing Animal Heroes

By Kelly Milner Halls

Turn the page for a sneak preview . . .

Lilly the pit bull is gentle and sweet. She loves to be scratched under her ears.

LOVE at First Sight

For Lilly, it started as an ordinary day. The five-year-old dog paced across her cage at the Animal Rescue League (sounds like LEEG) in Boston, Massachusetts. She ate her breakfast kibble. She curled up on her blanket to take short naps. Once in a while, she even barked with the other dogs. But she mostly seemed sad and lonely. Like the rest of the animals at the shelter, she needed a home.

That March morning in 2009 started out as a regular day for David Lanteigne (sounds like LAN-tane), too. But he was excited. He was going to do something new later that day. Something awesome. He was going to volunteer at the Animal Rescue League (ARL).

David is a police officer in Boston. He works five days a week helping people. On his day off, he wanted to help homeless dogs. At the shelter, David filled out the forms to become a volunteer. Then he asked if he could meet the canines (sounds

like KAY-nines). He meant the dogs.
Dogs belong to the group of animals
called canines.

"Sure," one of the ARL workers said.
"Come this way."

Slowly, David strolled past the cages.
He felt good about the job he had signed
up to do. All of the dogs needed loving
care, and he was just the guy to deliver it.
Then, six cages in, his heart skipped a
beat. He was face-to-face with Lilly.

"Hello, sweet girl," he said. Lilly's
golden eyes met his. "You have the most
beautiful eyes in the world," David told her.

Lilly calmly walked to the edge of her
cage where David waited. He gazed into
her gentle eyes. Then he noticed deep scars
on the dog's left side. There were scars on

the top of her head, too. *Lilly has been mistreated,* David thought. *What kind of person could hurt such a warmhearted dog?*

Lilly pressed her soft brown body against her cage to get closer to David. He felt like she was telling him, *I have been hurt, but I still know how to be good.*

David sat down beside the cage to talk to Lilly. "You *are* a good girl," he whispered. He stroked her fur through the cage. She liked it when he scratched her under her chin and behind her floppy ears. Her personality sparkled like a diamond.

"Can I walk one of the dogs?" David asked an ARL worker. "I think Lilly would like to go outside."

Lilly loved walking with David. They galloped through the grass and down the streets. She gave David dozens of sloppy licks. For man and dog, it was love at first sight. David realized he didn't just want to walk Lilly. He wanted to take her home.

To adopt Lilly, David needed to know if another dog and another person would love her, too. He had to introduce her to his dog, Penny. She's a golden retriever (sounds like ree-TREE-ver). David also wanted Lilly to meet his mom, Christine. David hoped Christine would share Lilly with him. He knew his mom got sad and lonely at times. He hoped taking care of Lilly would make her feel happier.

David drove to his mother's house. She lived about an hour away, in Shirley, Massachusetts. David told her about Lilly.

"Just meet her," he said. "Then you can decide if you like her as much as I do." Christine agreed to go meet Lilly.

Like David, Christine thought Lilly was beautiful. She was a little scared about walking her, though. Lilly is an American pit bull terrier (sounds like TER-ee-er), or pit bull for short. She weighs 70 pounds (32 kg). When she tugged at the leash, Christine could feel how strong she was. But Lilly seemed to understand Christine's fear. She quickly settled down.

Before they took Lilly back inside the shelter, David went to his car. Penny's dog biscuits were in the trunk. He wanted to share them with Lilly. When he popped the trunk open, Lilly jumped inside. She was ready to go home!

What Are Pit Bulls?

The first pit bulls were probably a cross between two kinds of dogs: the English bulldog and the Old English terrier. People in England created the breed about 200 years ago. The dogs were strong, smart, and loyal. They made excellent hunting dogs and watchdogs. In America, farmers used pit bulls to help protect cattle and sheep from wild animals. In the early 1900s, some pit bulls even looked after children. This earned them a special nickname. They were called "nanny dogs."

Want to know what happens next? Be sure to check out *Courageous Canine!*

INDEX

MORE INFORMATION

To find more information about the animal species featured in this book, check out these books, websites, and DVDs.

National Geographic Kids Everything Big Cats, National Geographic, 2011

National Geographic Readers: Sea Turtles, National Geographic, 2011

The Cornell Lab of Ornithology, "All About Birds: Common Loon,"
www.allaboutbirds.org/guide/Common_Loon/sounds

National Geographic, "Animals: Common Loon,"
animals.nationalgeographic.com/animals/birds/common-loon

National Geographic, "Animals: Green Sea Turtle,"
animals.nationalgeographic.com/animals/reptiles/green-turtle.html

National Geographic Kids, "Mammals: Clouded Leopards,"
video.nationalgeographic.com/video/kids/animals-pets-kids/mammals-kids/leopard-clouded-kids

Nat Geo Wild, "Return of the Clouded Leopards," DVD, 2013

This book is dedicated to the memory of my parents, Howard and Phoebe Alexander, who always believed I could do anything.

CREDITS

Cover, © IFAW/WTI S. Kadur; 4–5, © IFAW/WTI S. Kadur; 6, © IFAW/WTI A. Mookerjee; 15 (RT), © IFAW/WTI S. Kadur; 15 (LE), pjmalsbury/iStockphoto; 16, © IFAW/WTI A. Mookerjee; 22, Matt Gibson/Shutterstock; 26, ZSSD/Minden Pictures National Geographic Creative; 35, © IFAW/WTI S. Kadur; 36–37, Nadine Fuller; 38, Jim Rice; 45, burcintuncer/iStockphoto; 48, Nadine Fuller; 54, Isabellebonaire/Dreamstime; 58, richcarey/iStockphoto; 63, RonMasessa/iStockphoto; 68–69, PaulTessier/iStockphoto; 70, jimkruger/iStockphoto; 76, PaulTessier/iStockphoto; 80, Al Mueller/Shutterstock; 87, Lynn_Bystrom/iStockphoto; 90, Aline A. Newman; 96, Aline A. Newman; 101, Lindsay Dancy-LDancy Design and Co-founder of Lilly Fund Boston, MA; 102, © David R. Lanteigne; 109, Courtesy of Animal Farm Foundation; 111, © IFAW/WTI S. Kadur

ACKNOWLEDGMENTS

A special thank you to:

My husband, Neil, who helped me overcome a badly broken ankle to write this book

Ian Robinson and Sonali Ghosh, staunch defenders of clouded leopards and other wildlife

Nadine Fuller, Jim Rice, and James Burke, who rescued Koa and shared his story

Bob Zimmerman, Gary Lee, and Russ Brombacher, devoted Adirondackers and friends of loons

Hope Irvin Marston, Judy Ann Grant, Jule Lattimer, Jeanne Converse, and Jean Capron, past and present members of my writers' group

Regina Brooks, President of Serendipity Literary and my literary agent

The Old Forge Library and Isabella Worthen, Library Director, sponsors of 30-plus years of Old Forge Summer Writers Workshops

Marfé Ferguson Delano, eagle-eyed freelance project editor for National Geographic Children's Books

About the author: www.alinealexandernewman.com